dedicated to:
....
....
....

celebrating dogs

SHARE, REMEMBER, CHERISH

JIM McCANN, FOUNDER

celebrati●ns.com

**Andrews McMeel
Publishing, LLC**

Kansas City · Sydney · London

Andrews McMeel Publishing, LLC
an Andrews McMeel Universal company
1130 Walnut Street, Kansas City, Missouri 64106.

www.andrewsmcmeel.com

12 13 14 15 16 SMA 10 9 8 7 6 5 4 3 2 1

ISBN: 9781449427061

Library of Congress Control Number: 2012936741

ATTENTION: SCHOOLS AND BUSINESSES

Andrews McMeel books are available at quantity discounts with bulk purchase for
educational, business, or sales promotional use. For information, e-mail the Andrews
McMeel Publishing Special Sales Department: specialsales@amuniversal.com

Project manager and editor: Heidi Tyline King

Designed by Alexis Siroc

Produced by SMALLWOOD & STEWART, INC., NEW YORK CITY

Illustration credit information on page 70.

introduction

"JIM, YOU'VE GONE TO THE DOGS!"

"You're exactly right!" I replied. My colleague's comment about our latest book, *Celebrating Dogs*, made me chuckle. Indeed, the topic does seem like a departure from the other books in the *Celebrating...* series. We have covered milestone events and emotions—love, remembrance, graduation, and birthdays—but only two books have been devoted to a specific loved one: *Celebrating Mom* and now *Celebrating Dogs*. There is no denying it: The 1-800-Flowers.com family is a proud pack of treat-toting dog lovers.

Like other books in our *Celebrating...* series, *Celebrating Dogs* was born from all the great stories customers have shared with us

over the years about the special pets in their lives. The loyalty,

companionship, and yes, even the antics these furry friends

provide enrich our day-to-day living and help to make us

healthier and happier.

Of course, there is plenty of scientific research to back

up these claims, but I don't need research to know how nice it

feels to be greeted by a wiggly, tail-wagging bunch of fur at the end of a long day. Mickey, the current dog in my life, is a white West Highland Terrier and technically our "grand-dog." Mickey takes up residence with my wife and me whenever our son goes out of town. As empty-nesters, we enjoy the energy and love he brings to our house. I take more walks when Mickey is around—he insists—and I find myself sitting still to pet him—and sitting still is something that I don't do very often.

The biggest surprise of dog-sitting Mickey was discovering the network of dog lovers in our neighborhood. One morning, I took over my wife's duties and walked Mickey to the park at the end of our street. As we approached a group of unfamiliar neighbors, I heard someone say, *"Is that Mickey?"* Everyone and their dogs walked over to say hello, and because I was accompanying Mickey, I was immediately welcomed into the group. Talk about a four-legged icebreaker!

The same can be said for one of our most popular arrangements. Years ago, a customer suggested that we create a tribute to dog lovers. Since then, our *a-DOG-able®* arrangement has been a screaming success, no doubt because of the instant smiles that it gets upon delivery. It may seem kind of corny, but we feel honored to help our customers celebrate these deep, emotional connections. It's the same hope we have for *Celebrating Dogs*—that sharing the stories about your four-legged loved ones will help others express, connect, and celebrate the special pets and people in their lives.

Puppy Love

Is there anything sweeter than puppy breath?

—ANONYMOUS

Do you know what unconditional love is? It's being greeted each time I walk in the door with a sloppy lick from an excited dog—as if we had been separated for weeks as opposed to the five minutes it took me to carry out the trash. It's when I step on her paw by accident and she comes over to me to lick my hand as if to tell **me** that it's ok. It's when I forget to let her back inside—and she forgives me immediately for leaving her outside in the cold. *Unconditional love is the love of a dog.* —CHELSEA R.

Children are for people who can't have dogs.
—ANONYMOUS

After my sister died of brain cancer, my mother was understandably distraught, so we suggested she get a dog. And not just any dog—but a pound puppy that needed her help just as our sister had. At the shelter, she put her name on the wish list for a white Westie, the same type of dog she had always had.

"Mom," we laughed. "*Nobody* gets a Westie from the pound."

A week later, she received a call. A two-month-old white Westie was waiting for her. **Snowy,** as she named her, was more than Mom's companion for 12 years. She was truly a gift from our sister—sent straight from heaven. —JUDY M.

Top Breeds Around the World

United States	**Labrador Retriever**
France	**German Shepherd**
Germany	**German Shepherd**
Great Britain	**Labrador Retriever**

When Elton John married, his cocker spaniel, Arthur, served as best man at the ceremony.

Sometimes you don't get to choose your dog—it chooses you. I learned this firsthand when I decided to adopt a rescue dog from Hurricane Katrina. As I looked through the number of pets for **"Gigi,"** the name I had chosen, a little terrier caught my eye. As the volunteer brought her closer, tears began to well in my eyes. There, on a sticker taped to her collar, was the name, "Gigi," written in black marker. Needless to say, I took my little girl home. —JODY K.

puppy love

A French bulldog by the name of Olive cured my lifetime fear of dogs in just a few weeks. I had started a new job, and my colleague brought Olive in to the office each day. From day one, Olive set out to make me her new best friend, unaware that I was shrieking in fear—not because I wanted to play. She would seek me out and even made a habit of coming and sitting by my desk. Slowly, her lovable personality won me over, so much so that my fear of dogs is completely gone.

—SAM C.

Who can
believe that
there is no soul
behind those
luminous eyes!

—THÉOPHILE GAUTIER

It was unbearable to see so many unwanted dogs and puppies in the pound, but I forced myself to go in, consoled by the fact that I would rescue one. In the cage, eight puppies wagged their tails and licked my hands through the wire except one, the scrawny runt, huddled in the corner, afraid to even make eye contact. We chose her.

The next day, the pound called. All the puppies are being put to sleep, they said, because of a parvo outbreak.

"We're on our way!" I shouted into the phone. She was already ours, even if she wasn't yet home. Surviving parvo, two knee surgeries, and a host of other medical problems, she turned out to be not only as expensive as a full-bred but a priceless member of our family. —NANCY K.

Dog Et Al.

A Swedish researcher collected the DNA of 654 dogs around the world. He concluded that the entire population derived from a family tree of three Asian wolves from 15,000 years ago. South American dog fossils are genetically linked to Asian dogs, suggesting that when people migrated, they took their dogs along with them.

Every day when I would swim at my local health club, my guide dog, Princess, would walk up and down the pool deck beside me, no matter how many laps I swam. One day, however, the heat and appeal of the water were too much for her. She jumped in and swam the last lap with me. It was so cute—until I realized my cell phone was in the pouch attached to her harness. —NORINE L.

puppy love

My father always judged guests at our
house by the way our dog reacted to them.
If she didn't like them, then there was
good reason to be suspicious of them.

—CHRISTINA K.

two

Doggone It

The more one gets to
know of men, the more
one values dogs.

—ALPHONSE TOUSSENEL

**The most affectionate
creature in the world
is a wet dog.**

—AMBROSE BIERCE

I didn't need a dog, and I was sure of it after a weekend of dog sitting for my daughter. But there he was, on the morning news, and after two days I made the call to the pound to see if Raleigh was still available. Of course he was after all, few people line up to adopt a 12-year-old dog with missing teeth, a sensitive digestive system, cataracts, and a touch of arthritis that made him a bit grumpy.

Soon, I was researching foods to figure out what he could eat. I found myself sitting still for longer periods of time so that he could curl up in my lap. And my workouts increased—at first with his daily walk and later when I had to carry him up and down the stairs. In our short but so very sweet relationship, I learned that I needed Raleigh more than he needed me. —NANCY W.

How to bark in...

Spanish: Gau! Gau!

Swedish: Vov! Vov!

Indonesian: Gong! Gong!

Estonian: Auh-auh!

Cantonese: Wo! Wo!

Korean: Haw! Haw!

I was in a hurry and going too fast out of my neighborhood one morning when I accidentally hit a bird. The animal lover that I am, I assumed that it was only stunned, so I jumped out, scooped it up, and laid it on my lap, figuring that I'd drop it off at the wildlife shelter. As always, my Lab, **Milo**, was sitting in the front seat beside me. She sniffed the bird but didn't give it much attention, and we continued our drive into town. Just as I turned onto a busy road, the bird came to. It started flying around the inside of the car, and of course, Milo started chasing it. Even crazier, every time it would hit a window, bird droppings would fly. I pulled over as fast as I could and cracked the window enough for the bird to escape without Milo following suit. I took a deep breath then broke out into uncontrollable giggles. —MARTHA G.

Tabs, my miniature dachshund, stays with my sister during the week while I work. It's the perfect doggie daycare because our families live on 20 acres, giving her room to roam. A couple times a day, though, Tabs "runs away" to visit my brother-in-law. She begins by acting innocent, simply sitting in the yard. When my sister turns her head, Tabs moves a little farther away. The game continues until Tabs reaches the end of the drive, where she dashes full speed across the field. By the time she reaches my brother-in-law's office, her short legs have almost given out from the distance. But it's worth it. When she arrives, all the guys are waiting with a bowl of water and treats. —FAITH K.

We baby our scruffy little black terrier,
Skraggs—to the point that
someone once commented that
Skraggs won the lottery when he found
us. That may be true, but I think we
are the ones who won the jackpot.

—MARY S.

doggone it

We were traveling on the Interstate when my husband, Jay, and I spotted a big, beautiful golden retriever in the grassy divider between the busy north- and southbound lanes of traffic. We looked at each other, and at the next exit we turned around to try and help the dog. Pulling off the road, we realized that there were actually two dogs. The larger one, a male, was lying on top of a deceased female who had evidently been hit by a car. He would not leave her side. It took a lot of coaxing to get him into our car, and the stench was unbearable. It was obvious he had lain there, protecting her, for a day or two. When we got him to our vet, there was no microchip, and we had no luck in tracking down his owner. It was not in our plans to have another dog, but by the time retriever rescue showed up at our home a few days later, there was no way we were giving him away. We had **Renegade** for only a year after that, but this 100-pound golden teddy bear gave us enough love to last a lifetime. —CHERI K.

Who needs a shrink when there are dogs in the world?

—LAURIE W.

With a dog in your life, there is no such thing as a completely bad day. —MELISSA K.

doggone it

I was evaluating a suicidal child, and I was sure he needed to be hospitalized for intensive help. Knowing how anxious the mother and child were, I left my Lab, Santino, in the room with them while I reviewed his records. When I returned, the boy, his mom, and Santino were on the floor in a big huddle, hugging and cuddling each other. The love, security, and affection Santino gave them made it easier for them to accept my recommendation of hospitalization, and it gave them a small reprieve from their very real troubles. —NORINE L.

WHEN I WAS IN HIGH SCHOOL,
my dog always slept in his bed next to mine, but
when I tore a knee ligament, I had to camp out
downstairs. During the day he would sit with me,
but at night he would go upstairs to sleep, coming
down faithfully in the middle of the night when
he heard me moving about to take my medicine.
Only after I settled back into bed would he go back
upstairs. Up and down, up and down he would go,
convincing me that dogs can be some of our best
caretakers. —SHARON B.

When I was growing up, my stepfather, Tony, would go out for bagels on weekend mornings so that we could eat breakfast together as a family. Of course our dog, **Madison**, was included, and she would be given her own bagel to chew on for breakfast. Even after all us girls stopped eating bagels (too many carbs), Tony would go out and bring a bagel home for Madison.

—BROOKE B.

We celebrate our dog's birthday just like any other member of our family—with a special meal and a present or two. —LINDSEY E.

three

Canine Capers

*The dog was created especially
for children. He is the god of frolic.*

—HENRY WARD BEECHER

A dog running
through the field,
the sun on his back,
muddy ground
beneath his feet—
what could be a
better example of
pure joy? —CLAYTON C.

We had just finished the "free chicken dinner" I had gotten with a coupon from the local grocery, so I set the chicken carcass outside on the back porch for the cat to enjoy while I got the girls ready for bed. Thirty minutes later, when I came back downstairs, I noticed that someone had let Oliver, our dog, out on the porch—and the entire carcass was gone!

For the next two days, Oliver was lethargic. Worried, my husband insisted we take him to the vet just to make sure he was okay. He was okay, for sure *as in $700 okay* by the time we finished all the tests the vet recommended. It was the most expensive "free" chicken ever—and it cured me of couponing. —HEIDI K.

My childhood dog was a beagle, **Sundance the Kid,** and boy, did his name fit! Like the character from the movie, Sunny was mischievous and full of playfulness. We would play for hours, especially at bedtime, and when my mother would charge up the stairs to scold us for not being in bed, Sunny would bolt for his doggy bed, close his eyes, and feign sleep—leaving my sisters and me in the dog-house. It was a daily laugh for us and a memory that makes me laugh to this day. —SHARMY N.

I was intent on celebrating Maundy Thursday during Holy Week even though I was out of town for an intensive training session for the blind. In an unfamiliar church filled with the grave solemnity of the service, I reluctantly got up with my guide dog, Moses, and went forward to the altar for the traditional washing of the feet. There, at the front of the church, as a volunteer washed my feet, the silence was suddenly broken by a very loud "slurp, slurp." Apparently, Moses was thirsty and decided to drink the dirty water from the basin. It was a Maundy Thursday I will never forget. —NORINE L.

Did You Know...

Shortest Dog • Chihuahua • 8 inches

Tallest Dog • Irish Wolfhound • 32 inches

Heaviest Dog • English Mastiff • 175–225 pounds

Lightest Dog • Chihuahua • 5–6 pounds

The first organized dog show was held in England in 1859. The now famous Westminster dog show didn't begin until 1877.

It seems that even the most famous writers have had a dog eat their homework. The manuscript of *On the Road* by Jack Kerouac has a small notation next to a chewed edge at the bottom: "Ate by Patchkee, a dog."

When our Lab, Daisy Bell, was eight weeks old, a fox almost got the best of her out in our backyard. Fast forward ninety days later, she was playing outside, but when I called for her, she was nowhere to be found. About five minutes later, she ran out of the woods, stopped, and sat proudly upright—a long fox tail hanging out of her mouth. I couldn't understand what she said, but I think it was something like, "Dad, remember that fox when I was eight weeks old? Well, he should have gotten me when I was little!" —JIM B.

Canine Mascots

Some of today's biggest universities have a dog as their mascot:

University of Tennessee 🐾 Smokie 🐾 Bluetick Coonhound

University of Georgia 🐾 Uga 🐾 White Bulldog

Mississippi State University 🐾 Bully 🐾 Bulldog

University of Washington 🐾 Dubs 🐾 Alaskan Malamute

Carnegie Mellon University 🐾 Scottie 🐾 Scottish Terrier

It is unbelievable, but my daughter's hamster, Forrest, would ride around our house on the back of our Chihuahua, Sugarbear. Talk about the power of love shown through God's creatures great and small! —INELL F.

i had gone to Los Angeles for a job interview and was staying with friends who had just gotten a new puppy, Buster. The next morning, as my hosts were leaving, they warned me, **"Whatever you do, don't let Buster in the house."** As I made breakfast, Buster followed my every move, watching through the French windows and pleading to be let in. Finally, I was almost ready. What harm could it do? I opened the door and in flew Buster—over went the ironing board, my mug of coffee, and a bowl of flowers. A roll of paper towels unfurled as he ran upstairs and jumped onto my carefully pressed outfit. It took several minutes to corral him, and I arrived at the interview out of breath and a little disheveled. But Buster made me forget my anxiety, and I was offered the job the very next day. —CAROL B.

When **Maverick** was a puppy, he decided to redecorate the living room with an entire box of tissues he had shredded. When I walked in, he couldn't have been prouder. I remembered this story when a vet tech handed me a tissue the afternoon he crossed the Rainbow Bridge. The next day, I found a single tissue on the floor of my bedroom. It was as if he was telling me, "Mom, I'm okay. Don't worry; we'll meet again." —DEBBIE M.

I was petting a friend's dog

and listening to her sad tale of his abusive past before she rescued him.

"Is that how he got his scar?" I asked, pointing to a thin, circular scar around his snout. It looked as if his muzzle had been tied shut with wire or rope, leaving a permanent ring.

"Oh no," she laughed. "That is his war wound from aggressively licking the inside of the peanut butter jar. Having snatched it from the countertop, he shoved his snout inside and licked until all the peanut butter was gone. What he didn't realize is that the jar was cutting into his skin and making a permanent 'tattoo' as he licked." —HELEN K.

Smokey, half Irish setter and half Belgium sheepdog,
was an escape artist, but this time, it caught up with him.
He was hit by a car on Route 40, and my brother, Dean,
with tears in his eyes, pushed, carried, and coaxed him
home. The vet said he had internal injuries; there was
nothing he could do. We took him home, put him in the
laundry room, and he laid there for a week without eating
or getting up. We did force him to drink water. One day,
I went to check on him, and he was standing! His head was
down and his legs were unsteady, but he recovered and
lived another six years. That was plenty of time for him to
escape once again, turning up this time in a town five miles
away. When I went to pick him up, the policeman who
found him said he had been tied to a pole near the fire
house, even though his collar had a name and address.
I loaded him up and took him home.   —JOHN W.

my dad would always tell us stories of his dog growing up, a mangy, extremely ill-behaved collie they called Clancy. In northern Minnesota, outdoor activities are a source of great pride—especially those that take place in winter. So it should have come as no surprise to him when my grandma insisted he and Clancy compete in the Annual Hibbing Sled Dog Race at city hall.

Armed with a hot dog dangling from a string that was tied to the end of a stick, my dad dragged his mutt down to the starting line at city hall and, after some impressive negotiating, managed to get them both in place on time for the start. Just at that moment, poised for success but too anxious to wait for the gun, Clancy leapt into the air and, in the most athletic motion of his life, chomped the hot dog off the stick and laid down on the ground, never to cross even the starting line. —NELL R.

four

Man's Best Friend

The first time my husband and I left our shelter rescue, Ernie, at a kennel, we asked my dad to pick him up a few days early because we felt terrible about leaving him there. Since my dad and Ernie were great friends, we knew Ernie would love spending this extra time with my dad. This became the usual arrangement— Ernie didn't mind the kennel and we were guilt-free. Years later I learned my Dad would sleep in my parents' guest room so that Ernie could curl up next to him. My dad and Ernie had a special relationship, and even today thinking about the two of them together makes me smile. —ALEX S.

What better way to keep warm than to have a dog cuddled up against your back on a cold winter night? —NANCY W.

A house without either a cat or a dog is the house of a scoundrel.

—PORTUGUESE PROVERB

After our twelve-year-old Lab died, our house felt so lonely. To my husband's dismay, it was then that I had a realization: I may be able to live without a man, but I could never live without a dog.

—RUBY K.

My daughter's plans for a college roommate fell through, which meant that Julie would be living by herself. As a mother, I admit I was scared, even though her condo was close to the university. Then, just before she left for school, a friend called with news about a Yorkie at the pound whose time was running out. We raced to the shelter, and the moment we saw her, she ran to my daughters as if she had knew them. Yes, we kept her, and Marlee went away to school with Julie, helping her through a rough freshman year. To this day, they remain inseparable. And wouldn't you know, Marlee's affectionate personality was addictive. My youngest daughter insisted on a Yorkie for herself, and this fall, Sophie will be attending college with Caitlyn.

—JILL S.

When I was ten years old, I became sick with a serious stomach infection. Knowing instinctively that something was wrong with me, our family dog, **Morgan**, stood outside my bedroom door for five straight days. Later in his life, I was by his side when he passed away. —ERIK K.

We were worried about how our Lab mix would react when we brought our first baby home, but we should have known better. After watching us lay our daughter in the crib, Dixie stuck her nose through the crib bumpers, then promptly laid down. For the first few days, Dixie would get up only to eat and go outside, always returning to stand watch. When the baby cried, she would whimper. When my husband would walk the floors during late-night feedings, Dixie would follow three steps behind him. She remained devoted to our first daughter, and later, her two sisters, for the rest of her life. I have never understood how people can trade in the dog when the baby comes, because the dog was one of the greatest blessings our daughters have ever known. —PARIS K.

The Health Benefits of Being a Pet Owner

You've heard the hype, but there are many positive reasons for owing a pet. Among the most beneficial:

- Lower risk of allergies, asthma, and eczema

- A reduced chance of dying from a heart attack

- Increased physical activity

- Lower blood pressure

*The greatest love
is a mother's,
then a dog's,
then a sweetheart's.*

—POLISH PROVERB

The poodle is the national dog of France.

Raisin, my cairn terrier, has been

my constant companion since she was eight weeks old, but more recently, she has become my little angel. A couple of years ago, I was diagnosed with breast cancer. Through my surgeries, months of chemo treatments, and many restless nights on the couch, she was always at my feet. Sensing that something was wrong, she stayed steadfast throughout my fight, and her loyalty was such a comfort to me. Now, at 13, she is blind, and I feel privileged to be her angel and return all the unconditional love she gave me. —MALINDA H.

You think dogs will not be in heaven? I tell you, they will be there long before any of us.

—ROBERT LOUIS STEVENSON

When my wife left me for our neighbor, she took all our pets with her except our dog. April had refused to leave, digging her heels into the floor, resisting as my wife tried to pull her from the house. After that, April became protective of me, growling whenever she saw my ex, and even later, when I began dating and would bring lady friends to the house. Besides her unconditional love, April taught me another love—it's not so hard to be single when you have a faithful dog. —KARL Z.

When our beloved Airedale, **Walter**, died, the vet hospital accidentally sent his ashes to the oldest pet cemetery in the US, just north of NYC. We couldn't possibly bury him anywhere but underneath his favorite tree, so we went to pick up his ashes. Walking around made us realize the tremendous power that dogs—and all pets—have in people's lives. There were no formulaic inscriptions on the tombstones marking those tiny graves but instead heartfelt sentiments so poignant and consoling at the same time. Walter would have been in good company. —JOHN S.

The minute our new puppy, Chesa,

met my husband, Ken, the two were best friends. She was so eager to please him, and over the years she became a constant, obedient companion, always by his side. When Chesa was seven, however, she began an annoying habit of nudging Ken in the stomach and groin every time he sat down. No matter what he tried, he couldn't break her from it.

Three months later, Ken began having severe pains in that very area, and it dawned on us that perhaps Chesa was trying to tell him something. Sure enough, Ken was diagnosed with Stage 3 bladder cancer. Through 22 surgeries and countless trips to various specialists, Chesa stayed by Ken's side, her companionship never wavering. Ken has been cancer-free for seven years, and Chesa just died at age 14. Knowing he was safe, I truly believe, she felt she could finally leave him. —PORTIA P.

Mercy to animals means mercy to mankind.

—HENRY BERGH

illustration credits